Click here to see how you can visit the birthplace of Harry Potter and experience it in the most magical way possible: https://www.pottertrail.com.

While you're there, you might want to visit the most magical store around— the only place you could find more delightful curiosities would be Diagon Alley itself!

https://museumcontext.com

The Unofficial Potter Way of Solving Problems

How the Harry Potter Books Teach Us to
Deal with Difficult Situations

Olivia Kashti

THiNKaha®

E-mail: info@thinkaha.com
20660 Stevens Creek Blvd., Suite 210
Cupertino, CA 95014

Published by THiNKaha®
20660 Stevens Creek Blvd., Suite 210, Cupertino, CA 95014
http://thinkaha.com
E-mail: info@thinkaha.com

First Printing: July 2019
Hardcover ISBN: 978-1-61699-308-5   1-61699-308-1
Paperback ISBN: 978-1-61699-307-8   1-61699-307-3
eBook ISBN: 978-1-61699-306-1   1-61699-306-5
Place of Publication: Silicon Valley, California, USA
Library of Congress Number: 2018914520

Trademarks

All terms mentioned in this book that are known to be trademarks or service marks have been appropriately capitalized. Neither THiNKaha, nor any of its imprints, can attest to the accuracy of this information. Use of a term in this book should not be regarded as affecting the validity of any trademark or service mark.

Harry Potter is a registered trademark of Time Warner Entertainment Company.

This book is unofficial and unauthorized. It is not authorized, approved, licensed, or endorsed by J.K. Rowling, her publishers, or Time Warner Entertainment Company.

Warning and Disclaimer

Every effort has been made to make this book as complete and as accurate as possible. The information provided is on an "as is" basis. The author(s), publisher, and their agents assume no responsibility for errors or omissions. Nor do they assume liability or responsibility to any person or entity with respect to any loss or damages arising from the use of information contained herein.

Acknowledgements

To Richard Duffy and Will Naameh for being the weirdest people I know.

To the other Potter Trail guides for being great.

To Saher for supporting my brain.

To all of my Potter Trail guests who never stop being amazing.

To Mitchell Levy for liking my crazy.

To J.K. Rowling for starting it all.

To Harry Potter for being such a great guy.

To Mum and Abba for giving me a place to write.

To Ella, Sam, and Martha for being my sidekicks.

Dedication

For anybody who has ever identified themselves in a *Harry Potter* character, and anybody who has ever used *Harry Potter* to help themselves change.

How to Read a THiNKaha® Book

A Note from the Publisher

The AHAthat/THiNKaha series is the CliffsNotes of the 21st century. These books are contextual in nature. Although the actual words won't change, their meaning will every time you read one as your context will change. Be ready, you will experience your own AHA moments as you read the AHA messages™ in this book. They are designed to be stand-alone actionable messages that will help you think about a project you're working on, an event, a sales deal, a personal issue, etc. differently. As you read this book, please think about the following:

1. It should only take 15–20 minutes to read this book the first time out. When you're reading, write in the underlined area one to three action items that resonate with you.

2. Mark your calendar to re-read this book again in 30 days.

3. Repeat step #1 and mark one to three more AHA messages that resonate. They will most likely be different than the first time. BTW: this is also a great time to reflect on the AHAmessages that resonated with you during your last reading.

After reading a THiNKaha book, marking your AHA messages, re-reading it, and marking more AHA messages, you'll begin to see how these books contextually apply to you. AHAthat/THiNKaha books advocate for continuous, lifelong learning. They will help you transform your AHAs into actionable items with tangible results until you no longer have to say AHA to these moments—they'll become part of your daily practice as you continue to grow and learn.

Mitchell Levy, The AHA Guy at AHAthat
publisher@thinkaha.com

THiNKaha®

Contents

Introduction

At this point in time, it would be impossible to say how many people have read the Harry Potter books. Millions, at least. How many? It cannot be known. What kinds of people? Old, young, rich, poor, male, female, non-binary, etc. Where are these people from? What jobs do they have? What are their passions? None of these questions can be answered definitively. The Harry Potter books exist in seventy-four languages, so you can bet that all the people who have read the books have learned different lessons. But there is one thing that must be true for everyone who has imagined themselves in the halls of Hogwarts at one time or another: they have learned lessons.

Harry, Ron, Hermione and so many other characters we meet are faced with difficult issues. Sometimes they make mistakes, as we all do, but sometimes they find the best way of solving problems. In the end, they solve the biggest problem that the wizarding world is facing with hardly any experience or help—just by using their hearts and brains.

We can all find this kind of guidance through the *Harry Potter* books, whoever we are. *The Unofficial Potter Way of Solving Problems* helps make these lessons clear for us. It splits them into sections and reminds us of the ways that the books provide us with helpful advice on how best to solve problems in our own lives.

We can laugh as we remember Fred and George and their antics, we can cry as we think about the characters we lost, and we can smile fondly as we see all the ways in which love and friendship win in the end.

All of us have problems in our lives, and there is no better way to begin facing them and begin the huge challenge of working on ourselves than through reliving the magic of the Harry Potter World and remembering that as long as we stay good and true in our hearts and actions, Hogwarts will always be there to welcome us home.

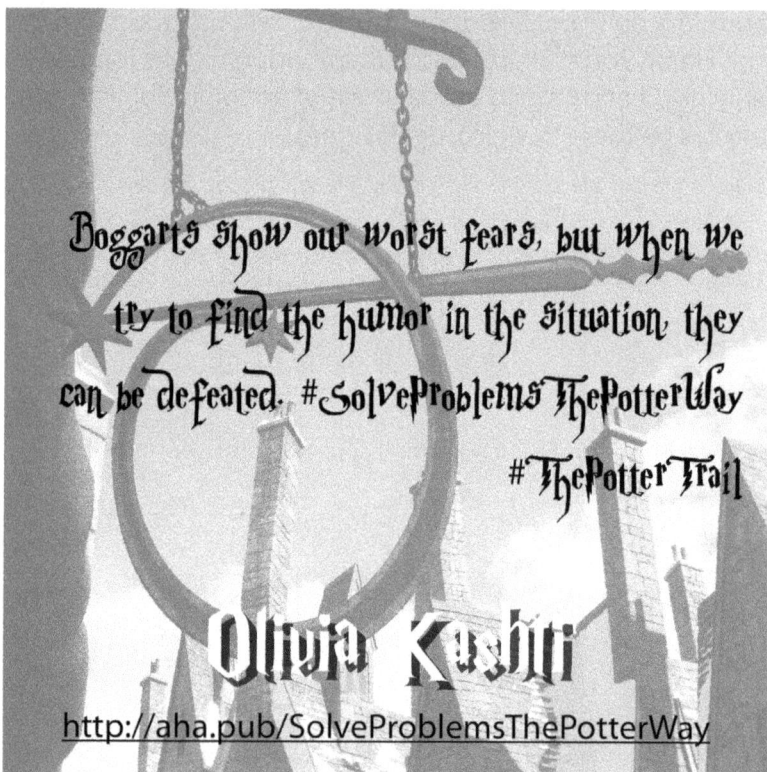

Boggarts show our worst fears, but when we try to find the humor in the situation they can be defeated. #SolveProblemsThePotterWay #ThePotterTrail

Olivia Kashti

http://aha.pub/SolveProblemsThePotterWay

Share the AHA messages from this book socially by going to http://aha.pub/SolveProblemsThePotterWay

Section I

Fear/Bravery

If Harry, Ron, and Hermione had simply run away from their problems instead of facing them, they would never have defeated the Dark Lord. Harry and his friends teach us that being brave pays off, whether it's in front of a Dementor, a friend you don't agree with, or the scariest of them all, a Boggart!

1

Harry does not allow intimidation to stop him from saying Voldemort's name. He knows he is fighting for good, and he will not give in to bullies. #SolveProblemsThePotterWay #ThePotterTrail

_____

_____

2

Ignoring problems doesn't make them go away; one must face them to achieve results. Often, fear of a problem is worse than the actual problem. #SolveProblemsThePotterWay #ThePotterTrail

_____

_____

3

"It takes a great deal of bravery to stand up to our enemies, but more to stand up to our friends." Neville proves we must stand up for our beliefs. #SolveProblemsThePotterWay #ThePotterTrail

_____

_____

_____

4

We all have the power to make our own
choices, despite the circumstances
we are born in, just like Harry.
#SolveProblemsThePotterWay
#ThePotterTrail

_____

_____

_____

5

Harry questions authority. Sometimes,
we must ask ourselves how we
feel in our hearts: Is something
right just because power tells us
so? #SolveProblemsThePotterWay
#ThePotterTrail

_____

_____

_____

6

Hermione has to erase her parents' memories to keep them safe. Sometimes we must do things we don't like, for the greater good. #SolveProblemsThePotterWay #ThePotterTrail

_____

_____

_____

7

Harry must fight in the Triwizard Cup despite not wanting to. He uses the skills he has — his broomstick, brain, and friends — to succeed. #SolveProblemsThePotterWay #ThePotterTrail

_____

_____

_____

8

Despite Harry being afraid of entering the Forbidden Forest, he knows that if he wants to help his friends, he must — so he does. #SolveProblemsThePotterWay #ThePotterTrail

_____

_____

_____

9

Harry finds solace in the Mirror of Erised, but with Dumbledore's help, he knows that "it does not do to dwell on dreams and forget to live." #SolveProblemsThePotterWay #ThePotterTrail

_____

_____

_____

10

Even though Harry knows nothing about magic when he joins Hogwarts, he puts in effort and becomes a good wizard. #SolveProblemsThePotterWay #ThePotterTrail

_____

_____

_____

11

Harry's bravery in the Chamber
of Secrets pays off, as he saves the
lives of Hermione and many others.
#SolveProblemsThePotterWay
#ThePotterTrail

_____

_____

_____

12

Boggarts show our worst fears, but
when we try to find the humor in
the situation, they can be defeated.
#SolveProblemsThePotterWay
#ThePotterTrail

_____

_____

_____

13

Our Patronus charms prove that when we remember all the positive things in our lives, the bad things can seem easier to deal with. #SolveProblemsThePotterWay #ThePotterTrail

_____

_____

_____

14

If you work in a team, everyone can share their skills to help each other, just like in Dumbledore's Army. #SolveProblemsThePotterWay #ThePotterTrail

_____

_____

_____

15

Even though Ginny is the only girl of all her siblings, she stands just as strong; don't let anything stop you from being yourself. #SolveProblemsThePotterWay #ThePotterTrail

_____

_____

_____

16

When Ron and Harry can't get through the gate at Platform 9¾, they use the flying car. Always look for alternatives before giving up! #SolveProblemsThePotterWay #ThePotterTrail

_____

_____

_____

17

People follow Voldemort because they are scared, but he leads them astray. Don't let fear guide you. #SolveProblemsThePotterWay #ThePotterTrail

_____

_____

_____

18

Sirius never stops trying to protect Harry, even though he risks his safety to do so. This makes him a role model in Harry's and our eyes. #SolveProblemsThePotterWay #ThePotterTrail

_____

_____

_____

19

The Dursleys run to an island in the middle of nowhere to escape their problems, but Hagrid finds them anyway. Don't run from your problems; face them. #SolveProblemsThePotterWay #ThePotterTrail

_____

_____

_____

20

Dementors can be fought by thinking happy thoughts. If you are brave and keep your calm, anything is possible. #SolveProblemsThePotterWay #ThePotterTrail

_____

_____

_____

When Ron and Hermione are fighting, Harry remains impartial. He knows he must be there for both his friends.
#SolveProblemsThePotterWay
#ThePotterTrail

Olivia Kashti

http://aha.pub/SolveProblemsThePotterWay

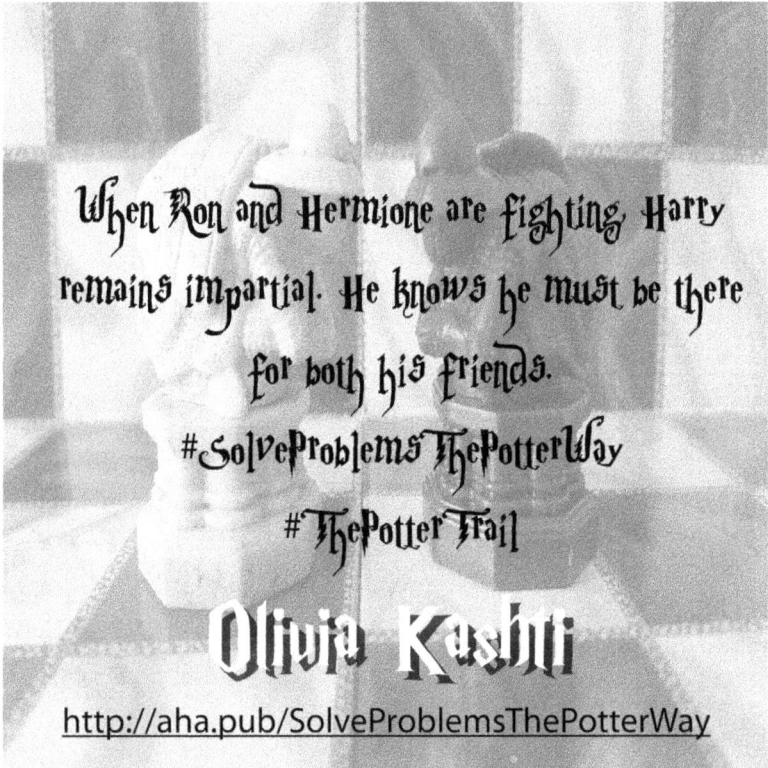

Share the AHA messages from this book socially by going to
http://aha.pub/SolveProblemsThePotterWay

Section II

Anger/Understanding

It's normal for witches and wizards to become angry when things don't go our way, but if Hogwarts has taught us anything, it's that keeping a cool head is the way to make progress. Being understanding and tolerant of ourselves and others means that problems can be solved quicker, leaving more time for fun at the end—this is what Fred and George think, anyway!

21

Hermione tells Harry that it is easier to forgive people for being wrong than being right. It is a big step, but one we must all take. #SolveProblemsThePotterWay #ThePotterTrail

_____

_____

_____

22

Just like Harry in the Chamber of Secrets, we can realize that we all make mistakes and have the capacity to grow. #SolveProblemsThePotterWay #ThePotterTrail

_____

_____

_____

23

At first, Harry does not want to accept that he is the Chosen One," but when he accepts his reality, he is able to achieve his potential. #SolveProblemsThePotterWay #ThePotterTrail

_____

_____

_____

24

Harry was angry about living with the Dursleys for many years, but otherwise, he would have been a celebrity from a young age. #SolveProblemsThePotterWay #ThePotterTrail

_____

_____

_____

25

Hippogriffs can sense anger and respond badly, so try to keep a positive attitude. #SolveProblemsThePotterWay #ThePotterTrail

_____

_____

_____

26

When Harry and George fight Malfoy
on the Quidditch pitch, they are punished.
Violence is not the way to deal with anger.
#SolveProblemsThePotterWay
#ThePotterTrail

_____

_____

_____

27

When Ron and Hermione are fighting,
Harry remains impartial. He knows he
must be there for both of his friends.
#SolveProblemsThePotterWay
#ThePotterTrail

_____

_____

_____

28

To fight Voldemort, Harry must realize that Voldemort is a part of who he is. Solving problems internally can help solve problems externally too. #SolveProblemsThePotterWay #ThePotterTrail

_____

_____

_____

29

Harry is angry that he has lost his parents, but when he most needs them, they return to help him. Be patient. #SolveProblemsThePotterWay #ThePotterTrail

_____

_____

_____

30

Hagrid is always understanding of Harry, and that is why they have such a close friendship. #SolveProblemsThePotterWay #ThePotterTrail

_____

_____

_____

31

Hagrid is understanding of all animals — that they are not evil just because they seem so. This makes his heart full of love. #SolveProblemsThePotterWay #ThePotterTrail

_____

_____

_____

32

Most werewolves follow Voldemort because they are shunned by the Wizard world. If more people understood them, they might not have turned bad. #SolveProblemsThePotterWay #ThePotterTrail

---

33

Thestrals are only seen by those who have witnessed death, but they can be useful. There is a silver lining to every situation. #SolveProblemsThePotterWay #ThePotterTrail

34

The relationships between goblins and wizards are strained because of misunderstandings. If both sides were honest, this wouldn't have happened. #SolveProblemsThePotterWay #ThePotterTrail

---

35

Wizards have tried to hunt giants out of existence, but if they tried to understand them, they could see that they are gentle and can help. #SolveProblemsThePotterWay #ThePotterTrail

36

Howlers display anger in card form,
so they aren't that nice, are they?
#SolveProblemsThePotterWay
#ThePotterTrail

_____
_____
_____

37

The Bloody Baron kills his love in anger,
then kills himself because he regrets
the actions he made when he was
angry. #SolveProblemsThePotterWay
#ThePotterTrail

_____
_____
_____

38

In Ron's anger, he attempts to curse Malfoy, but since his wand is broken, this backfires and he curses himself with slugs. #SolveProblemsThePotterWay #ThePotterTrail

_____

_____

_____

39

Ariana Dumbledore's father angrily attacks the Muggle boys that attacked his daughter, which leads to him spending time in Azkaban. #SolveProblemsThePotterWay #ThePotterTrail

_____

_____

_____

40

Harry's anger never serves as an ally for him, it only confuses him and makes things harder. Don't let anger rule you. #SolveProblemsThePotterWay #ThePotterTrail

_____

_____

_____

Harry could leave Malfoy to die in the Room of Requirement fire, but he does not. Just because others are evil, you don't have to be. #SolveProblemsThePotterWay

Olivia Kashti

http://aha.pub/SolveProblemsThePotterWay

Share the AHA messages from this book socially by going to
http://aha.pub/SolveProblemsThePotterWay

Section III

Rudeness/Honour

The good thing about the Potter characters we don't like is that they teach us what not to do—e.g., the rudeness of Malfoy, the Dursleys, and Kreacher. Instead, we look to characters who respect one another, keeping their honor and friendship. These build up strong relationships we admire, like the one between Harry and Dobby, and prove that keeping honor can help fix problems.

41

Malfoy calls others Mudblood, and in the end, he must ask for pity from Dumbledore because he is overwhelmed with the situation he has created. #SolveProblemsThePotterWay #ThePotterTrail

_____

_____

_____

42

Snape is rude to Harry because he misses Lily, Harry's mother. When people are rude, we must be kind; sometimes there is a reason behind it. #SolveProblemsThePotterWay #ThePotterTrail

_____

_____

_____

43

Harry could leave Malfoy to die in the Room of Requirement fire, but he does not. Just because others are evil, you don't have to be. #SolveProblemsThePotterWay #ThePotterTrail

_____

_____

_____

44

Ron offends Hermione at the Yule Ball because he is jealous that he is not her date. Think before you act: Why are you really being rude? #SolveProblemsThePotterWay #ThePotterTrail

---

45

Malfoy disrespects Buckbeak and gets injured because of it. Manners and respect cost nothing and can go a long way. #SolveProblemsThePotterWay #ThePotterTrail

---

46

Lockhart cares more about what people think of him than about people themselves. Look at where this gets him. #SolveProblemsThePotterWay #ThePotterTrail

_____

_____

_____

47

People are rude to Sybill Trelawney because she is eccentric, but she recites the prophesy that helps save the wizarding world. #SolveProblemsThePotterWay #ThePotterTrail

_____

_____

48

Hagrid is criticized for raising Aragog, but the acromantulas help fight Voldemort during the Battle of Hogwarts. Don't let others affect what you know to be true. #SolveProblemsThePotterWay #ThePotterTrail

_____

_____

_____

49

Great communication includes clarity. All that the house elves ask for is respect, and when this is returned, they help the wizards in every way they can. #SolveProblemsThePotterWay #ThePotterTrail

_____

_____

_____

50

Kreacher betrays Harry, but after Sirius is killed, he becomes Harry's servant. Stay loyal, or it can come back to haunt you. #SolveProblemsThePotterWay #ThePotterTrail

_____

_____

_____

51

Fawkes appears for Harry when he is needed. Help will always be there if you have earned it. #SolveProblemsThePotterWay #ThePotterTrail

---

52

Hogwarts will always be there for those who are loyal to it. #SolveProblemsThePotterWay #ThePotterTrail

53

The house elves are insulted by Hermione leaving clothes to free them. Respect how people want to be treated; don't force anything on them. #SolveProblemsThePotterWay #ThePotterTrail

_____

_____

_____

54

Ghosts are offended by the Ministry classing them as sentient creatures, so they receive a "Spirit Division." Respect everyone's differences. #SolveProblemsThePotterWay #ThePotterTrail

---

55

Peeves's rudeness earns him a reputation as the nuisance of school. Don't let this be you! #SolveProblemsThePotterWay #ThePotterTrail

56

The Dursleys are rude to the Wizarding community because they are scared of them, but ultimately, they realize they need their help to stay alive. #SolveProblemsThePotterWay #ThePotterTrail

_____

_____

_____

57

Hufflepuffs are known for their loyalty, one of their best character traits. #SolveProblemsThePotterWay #ThePotterTrail

_____

_____

_____

58

Ron and Harry are rude about Hermione, and she overhears, leading her to be trapped in a bathroom with a troll. Don't talk about friends behind their backs. #SolveProblemsThePotterWay #ThePotterTrail

_____

_____

_____

59

Hermione can be rude to her friends when she finds magic easier than they do (this is one of her bad qualities). Try to be kind and patient. #SolveProblemsThePotterWay #ThePotterTrail

_____

_____

_____

60

Aunt Marge is rude to Harry and ends up being blown up like a balloon. Being rude can come back to bite you in unexpected ways! #SolveProblemsThePotterWay #ThePotterTrail

_____

_____

_____

Romilda Vane uses a love potion to try and get Harry to love her, but in the end, she looks foolish. Trust that honesty will work out for you. #SolveProblemsThePotterWay #ThePotterTrail

Olivia Kashti

http://aha.pub/SolveProblemsThePotterWay

Share the AHA messages from this book socially by going to
http://aha.pub/SolveProblemsThePotterWay

Section IV

Lying/Honesty

Sometimes, lying can make things seem easier
to deal with, but as many Death Eaters know, it
doesn't solve problems. This section shows us how
telling the truth has the best results, proving why
honesty is always the best policy,
even without Veritaserum.

61

Lockhart's lies about his fame and fortune keep him afloat for a while, but when he is found out, he ends up losing everything, including his memory. #SolveProblemsThePotterWay #ThePotterTrail

---

62

Hagrid's accidental honesty helps Harry learn the truth about the Sorcerer's Stone. #SolveProblemsThePotterWay #ThePotterTrail

63

Harry doesn't tell anyone that Professor Umbridge is torturing him, but as soon as people find out, a solution is found. #SolveProblemsThePotterWay #ThePotterTrail

_____

_____

_____

64

Rita Skeeter lies about Harry's feelings and past, but since he knows he is being lied about, he stands up to her. #SolveProblemsThePotterWay #ThePotterTrail

_____

_____

_____

65

When Harry realises he knows Parseltongue, he lies about it. But when he understands what he can do with it, he uses this skill for good. #SolveProblemsThePotterWay #ThePotterTrail

----

66

Barty Crouch Jr. eventually gets found out for impersonating Mad Eye Moody. You can't keep a lie going forever. #SolveProblemsThePotterWay #ThePotterTrail

_____

_____

_____

67

Romilda Vane uses a love potion to try and get Harry to love her, but in the end, she looks foolish. Trust that honesty will work out for you. #SolveProblemsThePotterWay #ThePotterTrail

_____

_____

_____

68

Peter Pettigrew betrays his friends and turns to the Dark Side, but in the end, he is killed by his own betrayal. Stay loyal. #SolveProblemsThePotterWay #ThePotterTrail

_____

_____

_____

69

Obscurials try to hide their magical truth, but it turns them monstrous. Be honest about who you really are, and things will fall into place. #SolveProblemsThePotterWay #ThePotterTrail

_____

_____

_____

70

Ron doesn't talk to Harry because he thinks Harry has entered his name in the Goblet of Fire. If he had trusted Harry's honesty, he would not have fought with him. #SolveProblemsThePotterWay #ThePotterTrail

_____

_____

_____

71

The Daily Prophet calls Harry, "The Boy Who Lied," when he claims that Voldemort is back, and this stops people from believing the truth. #SolveProblemsThePotterWay #ThePotterTrail

_____

_____

_____

72

Harry knows Voldemort is a liar, so he stops believing him, and this helps him to fight the dark forces. #SolveProblemsThePotterWay #ThePotterTrail

---

73

Many people call Harry a liar, but it is because they are scared of the truth. Face the truth before accusing people. #SolveProblemsThePotterWay #ThePotterTrail

---

74

Sirius follows Harry around as an Animagus before revealing his true identity. If he had revealed it sooner, they may have had more time to bond. #SolveProblemsThePotterWay #ThePotterTrail

_____

_____

_____

75

Snape hid his true intentions his whole life. Had he been honest, perhaps people would have understood him more. #SolveProblemsThePotterWay #ThePotterTrail

_____

_____

_____

76

Peter Pettigrew lies to Harry rather than tell him the truth, so Harry loses trust in him. If you are not honest, people will not trust you. #SolveProblemsThePotterWay #ThePotterTrail

_____

_____

_____

77

The honest facts about the Chamber of Secrets were never given, so when the problem occurred again, people didn't know what to do. #SolveProblemsThePotterWay #ThePotterTrail

---

78

People find Luna strange because of her bluntness and honesty, but it shows that she is a person true of heart, and makes her a good friend. #SolveProblemsThePotterWay #ThePotterTrail

79

Lupin is always honest to Harry about what he knows, which helps Harry grow as a person. #SolveProblemsThePotterWay #ThePotterTrail

_____

_____

_____

80

Tom Riddle lies to Dumbledore about himself when they first meet, which means that Dumbledore cannot help him as he wants to. #SolveProblemsThePotterWay #ThePotterTrail

_____

_____

_____

Despite how often Dudley bullies Harry, he doesn't fight back. Harry knows that in the long run he will be a happier, better person. #SolveProblemsThePotterWay #ThePotterTrai

Olivia Kashti

http://aha.pub/SolveProblemsThePotterWay

Share the AHA messages from this book socially by going to
http://aha.pub/SolveProblemsThePotterWay

Section V

Bullying/Friendship

A problem shared is a problem halved, and Dumbledore's Army proves this. Sticking by the side of our friends, anything is possible—just ask Harry, Ron, and Hermione. Treating others badly will leave you alone and sad; there's a reason Tom Riddle ended up the way he did…

81

Despite how often Dudley bullies Harry, he doesn't fight back. Harry knows that in the long run, he will be a happier, better person. #SolveProblemsThePotterWay #ThePotterTrail

_____

_____

_____

82

Harry knows it is better to befriend Ron for friendship than Malfoy for money and bullying. #SolveProblemsThePotterWay #ThePotterTrail

---

83

Harry knows that if he asks for the help of his friends, it does not make him weak. It makes him strong and all of them strong together. #SolveProblemsThePotterWay #ThePotterTrail

---

84

Sirius teaches us that respect matters: "If you want to know what a man's like, take a good look at how he treats his inferiors, not his equals." #SolveProblemsThePotterWay #ThePotterTrail

_____

_____

_____

85

Harry saves Fleur's sister in the Triwizard Tournament challenge, so Fleur helps Harry. Using skills to help each other benefits all. #SolveProblemsThePotterWay #ThePotterTrail

_____

_____

_____

86

If it wasn't for the help of Hermione and Ron, Harry would never have been able to defeat the Dark Lord alone. #SolveProblemsThePotterWay #ThePotterTrail

_____

_____

_____

87

Harry and Voldemort fight because they are similar. Often, we are closer to our enemies than we think. Look for similarities, not differences. #SolveProblemsThePotterWay #ThePotterTrail

_____

_____

_____

88

When Luna is being bullied, she rises above it and does not suffer because of it. It is valuable to be able to turn the other cheek. #SolveProblemsThePotterWay #ThePotterTrail

_____

_____

_____

89

The Order of the Phoenix proves that if everybody works together, anything is possible. #SolveProblemsThePotterWay #ThePotterTrail

_____

_____

_____

90

When Dobby is slamming his head against a wall, Harry stops him. Friends must look out for one another — don't let friends hurt themselves. #SolveProblemsThePotterWay #ThePotterTrail

_____

_____

_____

91

Harry tells Voldemort: "You're the weak one, you will never know love or friendship. And I feel sorry for you." #SolveProblemsThePotterWay #ThePotterTrail

_____

_____

_____

92

Lily's love is the reason Harry stayed alive. Love is powerful. #SolveProblemsThePotterWay #ThePotterTrail

_____

_____

_____

93

When Uncle Vernon stops Harry from his Hogwarts letter, Harry persists and waits, and eventually, the letters come to him in hundreds. #SolveProblemsThePotterWay #ThePotterTrail

_____

_____

_____

94

Through Lupin giving Harry private DADA lessons, Harry can build his wizarding skills. Through using the advice of others, we can succeed. #SolveProblemsThePotterWay #ThePotterTrail

_____

_____

_____

95

The friendship that Harry and Hermione show to the house elves prove invaluable in their success against Voldemort. #SolveProblemsThePotterWay #ThePotterTrail

_____

_____

_____

96

The Malfoys, who bully Dobby, end up losing his trust and loyalty. #SolveProblemsThePotterWay #ThePotterTrail

_____

_____

_____

97

Stand up for yourself against bullies, and if there are older or wiser grown-ups around, like the Hogwarts professors, ask them for help. #SolveProblemsThePotterWay #ThePotterTrail

_____

_____

_____

98

If your heart is telling you that one situation is definitely right or wrong, listen to it — sometimes it knows. #SolveProblemsThePotterWay #ThePotterTrail

_____

_____

_____

99

Sometimes, the ways we react to bullies shows us our true talents — for example, Harry catching Neville's Remembrall that Malfoy throws. #SolveProblemsThePotterWay #ThePotterTrail

_____

_____

_____

100

Even though Aberforth is no longer friends with Albus, he still helps his pupils when he knows the time is right. Family bonds are strong. #SolveProblemsThePotterWay #ThePotterTrail

_____

_____

_____

Some leaders like Dumbledore are happy to share what they know; this sharing of knowledge helps all.
#SolveProblemsThePotterWay
#ThePotterTrail

Olivia Kashti

http://aha.pub/SolveProblemsThePotterWay

Share the AHA messages from this book socially by going to
http://aha.pub/SolveProblemsThePotterWay

Section VI

Greed/Sharing

Many characters in the Potter books are greedy, but they all have to pay the price for this. Other characters, like the Weasleys, choose to share everything, and end up united and strong enough to face whatever comes at them. Sharing is always the best way—except for, perhaps, when it's with a pack of Bertie Bott's Every Flavor Beans!

101

Malfoy uses blackmail and bribery to solve problems, but in the end, he is forced to face his demons and be held accountable for his actions. #SolveProblemsThePotterWay #ThePotterTrail

_____

_____

_____

102

Crabbe and Goyle eat the magic cakes they find floating around, which turn out to be filled with sleeping potions. Think before you take. #SolveProblemsThePotterWay #ThePotterTrail

_____

_____

_____

103

The Weasleys don't have a lot of means, but they still share because they wish to show love. #SolveProblemsThePotterWay #ThePotterTrail

_____

_____

_____

104

Mundungus Fletcher steals Sirius's belongings to sell, but he ends up giving away a Horcrux that could have stopped Voldemort. #SolveProblemsThePotterWay #ThePotterTrail

_____

_____

_____

105

Slughorn collects students he thinks will help him, but in the end, he puts people in danger for not valuing them for themselves. #SolveProblemsThePotterWay #ThePotterTrail

_____

_____

_____

106

Voldemort wants the whole Wizarding world for himself and other "purebloods," but this greed leads to his demise. #SolveProblemsThePotterWay #ThePotterTrail

_____

_____

_____

107

Some leaders like Dumbledore are happy to share what they know; this sharing of knowledge helps all. #SolveProblemsThePotterWay #ThePotterTrail

_____

_____

_____

108

Voldemort wants to keep all the magic for certain people, but this doesn't work. #SolveProblemsThePotterWay #ThePotterTrail

_____

_____

_____

109

Dudley steals some of Harry's birthday cake ... and he ends up with a pig tail! Sharing is caring. #SolveProblemsThePotterWay #ThePotterTrail

_____

_____

_____

110

Dudley demands one more present, and Petunia promises to buy this for him at the zoo, but once there, he ends up imprisoned in a snake pit! #SolveProblemsThePotterWay #ThePotterTrail

_____

_____

_____

111

Slughorn looks for talent rather than integrity. As a result, he ends up teaching Tom Riddle and helping him improve as a Dark wizard. #SolveProblemsThePotterWay #ThePotterTrail

_____

_____

_____

112

Helena Ravenclaw steals her mother's diadem and hides it and is then killed by the Bloody Baron. Don't steal; stay honest. #SolveProblemsThePotterWay #ThePotterTrail

_____

_____

_____

113

The Death Eaters were greedy for power but ended up on the wrong side of history. #SolveProblemsThePotterWay #ThePotterTrail

_____

_____

_____

114

Snape is greedy by arguing that Dumbledore should hide just Lily, not James and Harry too. His payback is only Harry surviving. #SolveProblemsThePotterWay #ThePotterTrail

---

115

The entrance to Gringotts: "Enter, stranger, but take heed of what awaits the sin of greed." People who steal from Gringotts are punished. #SolveProblemsThePotterWay #ThePotterTrail

116

Antioch Peverell, the original Elder
Wand owner, is greedy asking for
the most powerful wand in existence
and is the first of the brothers to
die. #SolveProblemsThePotterWay
#ThePotterTrail

_____

_____

_____

117

The owners of Borgin and Burkes are
known for being greedy for money,
and their greed helps Voldemort.
#SolveProblemsThePotterWay
#ThePotterTrail

_____

_____

_____

118

Xenophilius Lovegood is greedy for
just his daughter's safety, but this
puts the whole Wizarding world in
danger. #SolveProblemsThePotterWay
#ThePotterTrail

_____

_____

_____

119

Fred and George share the Marauder's Map with Harry, which ends up invaluably helping him defeat Dark magic. #SolveProblemsThePotterWay #ThePotterTrail

_____

_____

_____

120

Dumbledore shares the gift of the Invisibility Cloak with Harry, which ends up saving his life on multiple occasions. #SolveProblemsThePotterWay #ThePotterTrail

_____

_____

_____

Ron thinks Harry is trying to take Hermione from him, but this is the Horcrux manipulating his thoughts. Taking a step back from situations can help sometimes.
#SolveProblemsThePotterWay
#ThePotterTrail

Olivia Kashti

http://aha.pub/SolveProblemsThePotterWay

Share the AHA messages from this book socially by going to
http://aha.pub/SolveProblemsThePotterWay

Section VII

Jealousy/Forgiveness

Forgiveness is one of the hardest things to do, but when we forgive, we set ourselves and the other person free. Jealousy will just create misunderstanding; instead, we should lift our friends up so we can all be together. Relationships are important, and we must look after them just as closely as Filch looks after the halls of Hogwarts— although perhaps a bit less spookily!

121

Ron thinks Harry is trying to take Hermione from him, but this is the Horcrux manipulating his thoughts. Taking a step back from situations can help sometimes. #SolveProblemsThePotterWay #ThePotterTrail

_____

_____

_____

122

Snape wants the Defense Against the Dark Arts job, but the job is cursed. It's best that he trusts Dumbledore's decision. #SolveProblemsThePotterWay #ThePotterTrail

---

123

Ron is jealous of Victor Krum — he should have told Hermione how he felt and been honest with his feelings. #SolveProblemsThePotterWay #ThePotterTrail

---

124

Snape was antagonistic toward Harry, but he was jealous that he had never been able to be close with Lily. Forgiveness could have helped. #SolveProblemsThePotterWay #ThePotterTrail

---

125

Dumbledore forgives Malfoy for dealing with the Dark Arts, because he knows Malfoy is under pressure. #SolveProblemsThePotterWay #ThePotterTrail

---

126

Harry forgives Voldemort and pities him because he knows that Voldemort never had love in his life. #SolveProblemsThePotterWay #ThePotterTrail

---

127

Tonks forgives Lupin for whatever he does when he is a werewolf; she knows that he cannot control it. Be understanding. #SolveProblemsThePotterWay #ThePotterTrail

---

128

Even though Peeves is annoying most of the time, when the time comes, he helps fight Umbridge. #SolveProblemsThePotterWay #ThePotterTrail

---

129

Ron dates Padma Patil in response to his jealousy of Hermione with Victor, but this is not fair on Padma's feelings. Don't act on jealousy. #SolveProblemsThePotterWay #ThePotterTrail

---

130

Ron is jealous of Harry and Hermione being invited to Slughorn's party, but really, he should have been happy for his friends. #SolveProblemsThePotterWay #ThePotterTrail

_____

_____

_____

131

Draco is jealous of Harry's fame, but he fails to see the negatives that come with it. #SolveProblemsThePotterWay #ThePotterTrail

_____

_____

_____

132

Snape was always jealous of James Potter's talents, which meant they couldn't be friends. Don't let jealousy get in the way of friendships. #SolveProblemsThePotterWay #ThePotterTrail

_____

_____

_____

133

Cho Chang became jealous of Harry's friendship with Hermione, which damaged their relationship. Don't let this happen to you! #SolveProblemsThePotterWay #ThePotterTrail

_____

_____

_____

134

When Harry feels jealous of Ron for having a family, he tries not to be, as he knows that Ron is happy to share them with him. #SolveProblemsThePotterWay #ThePotterTrail

_____

_____

_____

135

Hagrid forgives all those who accuse him of bad things, meaning he is a happier, better person. #SolveProblemsThePotterWay #ThePotterTrail

_____

_____

_____

136

Instead of being jealous of Hermione's skills, Harry asks her for help and in turn, helps himself. #SolveProblemsThePotterWay #ThePotterTrail

_____

_____

_____

137

Sirius forgives Lupin for believing that he was a spy, and together, they work to try and stop Pettigrew. Forgiveness is key. #SolveProblemsThePotterWay #ThePotterTrail

_____

_____

_____

138

Instead of staying jealous of Harry, Ron decides to support him and knows that his own skills are worthwhile too. #SolveProblemsThePotterWay #ThePotterTrail

---

139

Filch is jealous of students for using magic when he is a Squib, but this means that his whole life is filled with bitterness. #SolveProblemsThePotterWay #ThePotterTrail

---

140

If someone is jealous of you, try to show them kindness, just like Harry and Dumbledore do, as this always works in your favor. #SolveProblemsThePotterWay #ThePotterTrail

_____

_____

_____

About the Author

Olivia Kashti is a Master's graduate, originally from Oxford, England. She now resides in Edinburgh where she works as a *Harry Potter* Tour Guide. Here, she has led thousands around the streets of Edinburgh, feeding them *Harry Potter* facts specific to the city, otherwise unknown. Olivia has always been a passionate writer, and her first degree in English literature helped develop this love of hers. Further studies in conflict resolution led her to see the benefit of written advice and help to those willing to seek it.

AHAthat™

THINKaha® has created AHAthat for you to share content from this book.

- Share each AHA message socially:
  http://aha.pub/SolveProblemsThePotterWay

- Share additional content: https://AHAthat.com

- Info on authoring: https://AHAthat.com/Author